1. **Introduction to Python**
   1.1   A Journey Through the History and Evolution of the Language
   1.2   Python Language Philosophy and Design
   1.3   Daily Use
   1.4   Installation and Setup of the Python Environment
2. **Language Fundamentals**
   - Basic Syntax and Data Types
   - Operators and Expressions
   - Control Structures: if, for, while
3. **Functions and Modules**
   - Defining and Calling Functions
   - Parameters and Returns
   - Organizing Code with Modules and Packages
4. **Working with Data**
   - String and File Manipulation
   - Collections: Lists, Tuples, Dictionaries, and Sets
   - List Comprehensions and Generator Expressions
5. **Object-Oriented Programming**
   - Classes and Objects
   - Inheritance and Polymorphism
   - Special Methods and Encapsulation
6. **Error Handling and Exceptions**
   - Understanding Exceptions
   - Handling Exceptions
   - Creating Custom Exceptions
7. **Interaction with the Operating System**
   - Shell Scripts and Automation
   - Accessing Files and Directories
   - Working with Processes and Threads

8. **Web Development with Python**
    - Web Frameworks: Flask and Django
    - MVC and Web Application Development
    - APIs and Web Services
9. **Data Science and Machine Learning**
    - Data Science Libraries: NumPy and pandas
    - Introduction to Machine Learning with scikit-learn
    - Data Visualization with Matplotlib and Seaborn
10. **Next Steps and Community Resources**
    - Best Practices and Coding Standards
    - Participating in the Python Community
    - Resources for Continued and Advanced Learning

Chapter 1: Introduction to Python

1.1: A Journey Through the History and Evolution of the Language

Created in the halls of the Center for Mathematics and Informatics (CWI) in the Netherlands in the last week of August 1989, Python Programming Language today is one of the greatest software ever written. Its creator, Guido van Rossum (also the creator of the ABC language), wanted to improve that language with some additional features, and to make the programming experience more natural and easier.

Python arrived on the scene in 1991 with its tongue firmly in its cheek. Its name was an affectionate reference to the surreal comedy group Monty Python. It was a conscious capitulation to levity and humour – as well as to a less authoritarian approach to programming – in the face of the earnestness of the wider programming world.

Readability was one of its earliest selling points, and Python's default emphasis on transparency has become another of its signature strengths. Programming languages that can more closely approximate human language – both in the readability of the code, and in its obvious syntax – allow the process of writing and reading code to feel almost immediate for many beginning programmers. With Python, this easiness of use is one of the language's most celebrated features. Learning Python is easy. This is a major selling point, when compared with any number of slightly more tangled programming languages. Its syntax is relatively accessible to developers at any level – one of many characteristics that make it welcoming to beginners. It's cheap to learn, and it's cheap to maintain over time.

Incrementalism that almost everyone has praised Each new version has been slightly better than the one before it: version 2.0, published in October 2000, featured list comprehensions and garbage collection. But 3.0, which shipped in December 2008, was a real milestone. The double diamond reflected deep changes in language design philosophy, eliminating some bad features in favour of improving others (notably a new string and I/O model). The break was controversial, and expensive: the codebase of Python 2 was huge, and needed maintenance for a long time while that for 3 was being built up. It was a very serious language, easy to use for any enterprise project. Controversy soon abated, though: the change settled in, and 2.x was kept alive through huge extensions of support patches before it was retired in 2020.

It has been powered by a philosophy of open, collaborative development, where the language's change governed by user feedback, and a corresponding set of libraries and frameworks in nearly any area you can think of (particularly in web development, but also in data science, AI and more).

Through its many guises, Python has given the impression of a program that was, and is, high-level, human-sounding and powerful, one that was, and is, perpetually and consistently augmented by a vibrant, active and responsive community, and one that was, and is, forever propped up by an amazing collection of modules and tools. Python today is, in effect, a one-stop toolshop for scientists, engineers and programmers of every flavour, a general-purpose Swiss Army knife for getting things done, and a marvel of ingenuity.

1.2: Python Language Philosophy and Design

Python's guiding philosophy embraces the explicit, the simple, and the clear: read the 'Zen of Python', a series of 19 'affirmations' about the design of Python, or better still write Python, because Zen is a terse list of Python's stylistic eccentricities – the quirks that make it workable, quirky and effective, in form as much as in content:

1. Be explicit rather than implicit. One of Python's design tenets, for example, is an injunction to be explicit. Hence its 'encouraging' developers to write self explicitly when constructing object methods – a use of self that signals, explicitly, that the message is being sent to the instance itself.

2. In all things, the extension principle is better than the restriction principle. In all things, simplicity is better than complexity. The syntax of Python should be as easy to read and as easy to express in human-sounding text as possible. This goal of simplicity should never be confused with lack of power – on the contrary, the simplicity in Python ultimately makes it easier to conduct and maintain code, especially in a scholarly and research-driven environment that relies on academic collaboration.

3. Complex not complicated. Though we love the simple in style, the language isn't afraid to showcase complex solutions to problems, but complex should never turn into complicated and obscure.

4. It's all about readability. The most subversive aspect of Python is its obsession with readability. Coding style – two spaces, not tabs, for indentation – isn't an idiosyncrasy or a matter of personal preference, but a syntactical requirement, enforced to help guarantee a kind of uniformity that makes life easier not just for beginners but for experts as well.

And this is reflected in the way Python itself was designed with this same spirit of extendability and modularity in mind — meaning that it supports packages ('namespaces' and reusable containers of entire libraries of code) and modules (namespaces and reusable containers of individual chunks of code), and also is intentionally 'glue' intended to combine with other languages and other codebase chunks (with extensive support for system calls and other libraries).

Python's type system is dynamic and strong – that is, it doesn't require explicit type declarations, like statically typed languages do – and this is usually part of the reason why Python code can be so short and readable. Python's type system is dynamic and strong – that is, it doesn't require explicit type declarations, like statically typed languages do – and this is usually part of the reason why Python code can be so short and readable Nevertheless, since Python version 3.5, it has had the option of allowing some type annotations, helping with type-checking at development time, improving readability and robustness.

There is also the way Python handles memory. It's worth remarking on that too. The name Python refers to the Python interpreter, of which there are several implementations; CPython is the most well-known and the most common, because it runs in the C programming language, and it does two clever things to handle memory automatically using a process called reference counting and garbage collection which, to state the obvious, further abstracts one of the most daunting and bug-happy tasks in programming: memory management.

Finally, Python is pragmatic in the sense that it encourages specific styles and modes of thinking about things, but it leaves the implementation alone: it is easy to write Python, easy to maintain Python, and this ease leads to a reduced level of frustration when designing and implementing solutions. It is a 'gentle' language, providing the scaffolding or the way of thinking when solving a problem, while leaving the door open to several ways of completing the job. Python supports multiple programming paradigms: procedural programming, object-oriented programming, and functional programming, to name a few.

The philosophy of Python (egalitarian, exuberant, embracing of change) has helped to make the language one of the most popular in the world, but it's also an example of a development model that provides a sensible balance of power and ease of use – and that's part of Python's extraordinary maturity, too.

1.3: Daily Use

Web Development: Under the hood of many modern web applications is Python. Frameworks like Django and Flask are used to build and to control websites – to manage requests from clients (such as your web browser), and to handle the logic of accessing databases, server-side logic and user input. They add a lot of utility to the language for developers, enabling them to quickly create robust, scalable web applications.

Data Analysis: Business applications of Python include data analysis, which is by far the most common use of the language within this domain. Python is chiefly used in this context by means of libraries such as pandas, a tool used primarily for parsing, processing and displaying data for the purposes of gaining insight and informing decisions, and NumPy, which is a Python-based development of Numerical Python, a package commonly used for scientific computing and engineering. Again, the reasons that Python is favoured as a means of facilitating these analyses are very similar to those mentioned above: Python is simple to learn and easy to read. Data scientists who work with large datasets and perform complex analyses can benefit from using Python for these tasks.

Artificial Intelligence (AI) and Machine Learning (ML): Most of the modern AI and ML apps that power our modern lives, from chatbots for casual conversation to more advanced recommendation engines on popular streaming media platforms, are actually built using Python. AI and ML apps require some implementation of machine learning libraries such as TensorFlow and Keras to create models that can 'learn' from data and make decisions on what's seen or detected. Python has some of the most robust libraries of any programming language for building, deploying and scaling these complex models to solve problems or meet user needs based on data.

Finance: Python is used extensively in finance for algorithmic and high-frequency trading, portfolio and risk management. Raw speed and ability to process large sets of data, plus the existence of versatile, well-curated libraries for statistical computations, makes it a favourite tool of quantitative analysts. Being able to wrangle and analyse large data sets quickly is a major boon to the financial world.

Scientific computing: Python's vast libraries may also be used in scientific research, as one can use the same language to perform an experiment, analyse the data, and carry out any number of other complicated computations a quantum computer can do. Libraries such as SciPy and Biopython offer tools for use in scientific applications, making Python a valuable tool in research.

Programming and intro to problem-solving Python's simple syntax and readability make it a popular language for teaching programming and intro to problem-solving. Experienced developers often criticise students coming into the field for lacking fundamental knowledge of datatypes like strings, numbers, lists or arrays. Python is one of the easiest languages to learn, with simple syntax that may be read as though it were written in human-sounding text. New programmers can quickly grasp fundamental concepts that will benefit them for years to come.

Software Development: Besides web applications, Python is used for building desktop applications, computer games and other software. PyQt and Tkinter are two of the most popular libraries for building graphical user interfaces, while Pygame is used for game development. Python and its extensive libraries are very versatile, making it suitable for a great many software development projects.

Automation: Administrative tasks like file management, system updates, and network configuration can be automated through Python scripts. This is helpful because you don't need to do the same tasks manually, and automating repetitive work makes these tasks much quicker and less prone to human error. Python's scripting ease and useful libraries make automation work.

Internet of Things (IoT): Another place where we occasionally see Python showing up is in the Internet of Things (IoT), where it's used to write scripts that you run on a device to drive it (often either a Raspberry Pi or an Arduino). The scripts allow a device to gather data, communicate and exchange information with other devices, and execute some basic tasks. The simplicity and versatility of Python make it a good option for IoT application development.

Operating Systems: Various Linux distributions use Python to configure and administer. Lot of system administrator tools have been scripted in Python to help manage users, manage disks, etc. Python is a great tool for system administration because of its flexibility and its large library of tools.

Entertainment: In the entertainment industry, Python is used to script the handiwork of animating multiple characters and objects inside animation software and game engines by thousands, resulting in faster production time. Its ability to computationally handle complexity makes Python an efficient tool for film and game production.

Healthcare: Python has many applications in healthcare, e.g. analysing large datasets, making predictions, and aiding diagnosis through analysis of medical imaging. Python can analyse healthcare trends and could potentially be used to help with diagnoses and treatment planning. Healthcare applications and research are best conducted using Python, since it has the largest number of libraries and frameworks.

All of these applications are built on top of Python's ease of use, abundant libraries and thriving community, making it a key piece of technology infrastructure helping to enrich and sustain our lives in a myriad of visible and invisible ways.

1.4: Installation and Setup of the Python Environment

If you install the Python programming language for the first time on a Mac OS, Windows or Linux operating system, you need to take into account the differences between these systems. Instructions on how to proceed are somewhat differently represented: Anybody who instals any of these operating systems must first determine whether Python is already installed (especially on macOS which comes with Python by default).

This is also (needless to say) true for the install instructions for macOS/Linux and Windows, where the first instruction of the installation process is to go to the website of Python, so that one can obtain the official version of Python (since this is the cross-platform way of obtaining the Python interpreter).

This means that installing Python is going to be different depending on the operating-system environment (macOS, Windows, and Linux) in which you're running it. For Mac users who already have the system Python installed, installing Python – by which I mean installing Python for Google Cloud – can be done through the free, open-source package manager Homebrew, which can install third-party Mac software more easily than is possible through macOS itself. But because there are already two systems in play (one Python that's already pre-installed in the Mac, and a second one, which is to say, the Python install you're instructed to do), the install instructions on macOS warn the user – as do the macOS/Linux install instructions and the Windows install instructions – not to run install commands in the same environment with the system Python pre-installed in macOS, or with any version of macOS you want to re-image/restore your Mac system to. Because you already have Python installed with macOS: you want to isolate your install for Homebrew. Because those macOS 'isolating' install instructions are rhetorically prominent, that move is repeated in the macOS/Linux install instructions and in the Windows install instructions.

These directions similarly encourage their users to create a Python 'virtual environment' for any given project, not interfering (or being interfered with) by (or by) any potential system-wide Python installation, and enclosing any project development within this sandbox.

As soon as you pick up the first word of that task, to do anything more sophisticated than writing (and hopefully running) Python code, you'll have to set up a Python programming environment, such as downloading a Python interpreter to the target machine, configuring the right code editor or IDE (integrated development environment), and managing libraries and dependencies.

Step 1: Installing Python

Windows, macOS, and Linux:

Download Python:

• Visit the official Python website at www.python.org.
• Go to "Downloads" section. The site automatically suggests the preferable version for your OS.
• For Windows and macOS, download the installer. For Linux, it might be available directly through the package manager.

Run the Installer:

• Windows: Run the downloaded executable. Be sure to tick the box that says 'Add Python 3.x to PATH' before clicking 'Install Now'. This is very important, as it puts Python in a place where you can access it from the command line.

• macOS: Open the downloaded .pkg file and follow the instructions to install Python.

• Linux: Python is often pre-installed. If not, it can be installed via the package manager. For instance, on Ubuntu you might use command:

```
sudo apt update
sudo apt install python3
```

Verify Installation:

• Open your command line interface (Command Prompt on Windows, Terminal on macOS and Linux) and type the following command:

```
python --version
```

That must return the current version of Python installed, confirming the installation.

Step 2: Setting Up an IDE or Code Editor

While it's possible to code in Python using only a simple text editor, an IDE can greatly improve the coding experience thanks to features like syntax highlighting, auto-completion of code, and debugging tools.

Popular Python IDEs and Editors:

• PyCharm: By JetBrains, this is the most sophisticated IDE for Python, with lots of features to offer for beginners and advanced users alike. The free Community Edition and paid Professional Edition.

• Visual Studio Code (VS Code): A fast and lightweight source code editor with Python support added by extensions such as the Python extension from Microsoft (see figure below), including native debugging, embedded Git control, syntax highlighting, smart code completion, snippets and code refactoring.

- Jupyter Notebook: Perfect for data science and learning. Create and share documents with live code, equations, visualisations and narrative text.

To install an IDE:

- From the official site, download the installer (for PyCharm, go to jetbrains.com/pycharm/; for VS Code, go to code.visualstudio.com).
- Run the installer and follow the on-screen instructions.

Step 3: Managing Packages with pip

Python uses pip (Python's package installer) to manage software libraries:

- Install a Package:

    pip install package_name

- **List installed packages**:

    pip list

- **Upgrade a package**:

    pip install --upgrade package_name

Step 4: Virtual Environments

Using virtual environments can be an easy way of ensuring that dependencies for projects are properly managed, eliminating conflicts about package versions.

Creating a Virtual Environment:

• Install virtualenv if it's not installed:

pip install virtualenv

• Create a virtual environment:

virtualenv myenv

• Activate the virtual environment:
- Windows:

.\myenv\Scripts\activate

- macOS and Linux:

source myenv/bin/activate

By following all these previous steps, you will create a robust Python programming environment set up on your machine, capable of handling basic scripts to complex applications.

Chapter 2: Language Fundamentals

In this chapter, we start at the beginning. You will learn Python's syntax – the formal structures, the 'language grammar', on which every line of every Python program depends. Understanding Python's syntax is the fundamental requirement of writing clean, readable and dependable programs that actually do what you want them to do – and that are also easy to maintain and update over time.

2.1 Basic Syntax and Data Types

At first glance, Python's syntax is a bit alien – deliberately so, because it wants to be unnatural and unintuitive, so that it's easy to read. And yes, it's really that weird. Python's design philosophy, which states simply 'Readability counts', demands that every line of source code be readable by a human, not just a machine, so that the software works not only now but also for the developer who has to work with it in the future.

Key Syntax Features:

• Indentation: Python uses indentation to define a code block, rather than curly braces {}. This requirement is imposed because, unlike most programming languages, indentation is visually essential not only for readability but also for maintainability. In Python, proper indentation is not an aesthetic afterthought; it determines script execution – everything else comes second.

• Comments: Comments in Python start with the hash mark (#). The purpose of a comment is to clarify what the code is supposed to do. It's helpful for the author, months after they wrote a particular section of code, or could be helpful to other readers of your code. Good commenting practices will make your code more understandable to others. This will make it easier for you to maintain and fix bugs as you go.

Core Data Types:

• Numerics: Python is equipped with a number of different numeric types: integers (int), floating-point numbers (float), and complex numbers (complex). Each of these data types can be used for different types of mathematical operations (e.g., integers for counting; floats for exact arithmetic; complex numbers for complex algebra).

• Strings: In Python, text is treated as a string. A string is a sequence of characters defined by a pair of single or double quotes. Like strings in many other programming languages, strings in Python are immutable. This means that you can't alter a string once it's created, even though you can do a lot of other things to it and create new strings from the results.

• Booleans: Python has Boolean values (True and False) used to test if a condition is met. Boolean expressions are the basis for making choices in the code, steering the flow of execution depending on whether some condition is met or not.

• Lists, Tuples, and Dictionaries:

• Lists: mutable sequences, best for storing collections of things where it's usually necessary to change what's in the collection.

- Tuples: Immutable sequences, perfect for storing fixed collections of items.

- Dictionaries: Key-value stores that excel in scenarios requiring fast lookup, insertion, and deletion operations.

2.2 Operators and Expressions

Operators are a type of special syntax in Python that, along with values and variables, make up an expression.

Operator Types:

- Arithmetic Operators: Perform mathematical calculations like addition (+), subtraction (-), multiplication (*), and division (/).

- Comparison operators: Check the relationship between two values, such as equality (==) and inequality (!=), and greater than or lesser than relationships (>, <, <=, >=).

- Logical Operators: Combine Boolean expressions logically with and, or, and not.

- Assignment Operators: Assigns variables values – with assignment operators such as simple, or direct assignment (=), add (+=), subtract (-=), mutliply (*=) and divide (/=).

- Expressions: A sequence of elements (combinations of variables, constants and operators) that Python evaluates to produce a value. These help us combine more complex calculations and conditions into expressions that reduce the number of lines of code required and improve performance.

2.3 Control Structures: if, for, while

Control structures control the flow of program execution, and thus they are as essential to creating responsive and elegant Python programs as they are to programs written in any other language.

• if statements (if, elif, else): execute code depending on certain conditions; the most basic form of decision-making in Python; a similar structure to if, then, else in other languages, and absolutely indispensable to performing conditional logic in any program.

• Loops:

• For Loop: Iterates once (or more than once) over a sequence (list, tuple, string, etc), executing a block of code for each item in the sequence.

• Loop: Runs as long as a condition is true, often useful when you don't know in advance how many times to run.

• Control Flow Modifiers: break and continue modify the execution of loops, where break terminates the loop and continue jumps to the next iteration. An else clause after a loop executes code once when the loop condition becomes False – unless the loop was prematurely terminated by break.

This chapter includes everything you must know to be able to start writing useful Python programs: if it isn't here, it couldn't be important enough. It covers the rules for the logical structure of your code.

Chapter 3: Functions and Modules

This chapter tackles one of the most powerful features of Python: we are going to learn how to write functions and modules – ways of reusing your own code in your own programs and organising your code into modules and packages. If you can write functions and create structures consisting of modules and packages, you will be ready to start a modular Python project.

3.1 Defining and Calling Functions

Having reusable code is the real benefit of functions, the core building block of Python programs. A Python function consists of the keyword def, the function name, a pair of parentheses that might contain parameters, a colon that marks the start of the body of the function, and the body itself.

Functions are the means of achieving reuse, modularity and clarity in Python code. A function is something that we define with the keyword def to encapsulate some code for some task in a block so that we can execute it as needed.

Defining a Function:

• Syntax: A function definition starts with the def keyword, followed by the function name and opening parentheses. Any arguments that the function takes as input are written inside the parentheses. The function block is indented to the right after the colon.

```
def add(a, b):
    return a + b
```

This simple function add takes two parameters and returns their sum.

• Docstrings: Right underneath the function signature, a docstring (documentation string) describes what the function will do, what it takes as input, and what it returns. This is important from a maintainability and readability standpoint.

```
def greet(name):
    """Greet someone by their name."""
    print(f"Hello, {name}!")
```

• To perform a function, use the function name followed by parentheses. If the function expects arguments, you put the arguments inside these parentheses.

```
result = add(5, 3)
print(result)  # Outputs: 8
greet("Alice")  # Outputs: Hello, Alice!
```

3.2 Parameters and Returns

Functions can take parameters, ie variables that are passed into the function, and return a value to the caller via a return statement.

Parameters and return values enable functions to accept inputs and generate outputs, and that's it.

Everything in any programming task you could ever imagine can be accomplished using these tools.

Parameters:

• Positional Parameters: Passed to functions in the order they are defined in, they are the most common sort of parameter.

• Keyword Parameters: Parameters that are passed by giving each one an explicit name in the function call; this makes the pass-through clear and independent of the order of the parameters.

• Default parameters: Parameters that have a default value, which will be used if no argument is supplied for that parameter when calling a function. This makes some arguments optional.

```
def power(base, exponent=2):
    return base ** exponent
print(power(3))  # Outputs: 9, using the default exponent
```

Returns:

• Returns a value (a return value) using the return statement. When no return is explicit, it returns None.

• Functions deliver results back to the caller through the return statement. If no return statement is included, none isset to the return value of all Python functions by default.

```
def multiply(x, y):
    return x * y
```

3.3 Organizing Code with Modules and Packages

Modules and packages are how you organise larger Python projects. A module is just any file with suffix .py that has some Python code in it, and a package is any directory that contains multiple modules and another module named __init__.py.

Modules:

• A Python module is a file (ending with .py) containing Python definitions and statements. It can contain definitions of functions, classes and variables that can be reused in other Python scripts.

• Importing: Modules are imported with the import statement. Attributes or functions can be imported individually with the from keyword.

• You can wrap your code into a module by saving it into a new file, with a .py extension. Other Python scripts can then import this module to use functions and variables defined inside.

```
# Assuming add and multiply are defined in math_operations.py
from math_operations import add, multiply
```

Packages:

• A package is a directory with an __init__.py file containing a group of modules, some of which can be other packages (making for a hierarchical package namespace), and that is used to organise a collection of modules. This information suggests that building a package is the process of creating a directory with an __init__.py file and throwing modules into it.

• Hierarchical Structure: modules in a package can be organised in a nice hierarchical way along with namespace management through dot notation Packages provide a module namespace hierarchical organisation through dot notation. For example, a module module.py can be placed in a package package and become package.module. See the example:

```
# File structure
# - mypackage/
#   - __init__.py
#   - submodule.py
# Importing from a package
from mypackage import submodule
```

Using functions, modules and packages effectively will help you write some of the most readable, most efficient and most modular Python code you can. It will keep your work area relatively clean, and, as applications grow, it will keep the number of dependencies and namespaces that can cause headaches to a manageable amount.

Chapter 4: Working with Data

The chapter centred on Python's programming capabilities for data manipulation, with emphasis on operations on strings, working with files, and more advanced data structures such as lists, tuples, dictionaries and sets.

4.1 String and File Manipulation

Strings are one of the most frequently used data types in Python and serve as the core of many data-processing workflows.

String Operations:

- Basic Operations: Includes accessing characters, slicing strings, and concatenating strings using the + operator.

```
s = "Hello, world!"
print(s[1])  # e
print(s[7:12])  # world
greeting = "Hello" + " " + "Python!"
print(greeting)  # Hello Python!
```

- Methods: strings in Python have built-in methods such as .upper(), .lower(), .strip(), .split(), and .replace() that allow for formatting, searching, and changing strings.

```
phrase = " Hello, Python! "
print(phrase.upper())  # HELLO, PYTHON!
print(phrase.lower())  # hello, python!
print(phrase.strip())  # "Hello, Python!"
print(phrase.split(','))  # [' Hello', ' Python! ']
print(phrase.replace('Python', 'World'))  # " Hello, World! "
```

- Formatting: Python has many ways to format strings, most notably the f-strings for embedding expressions inside string literals that were added in Python 3.6.

```
name = "Alice"
age = 30
greeting = f"Hello, {name}. You are {age} years old."
```

print(greeting) # Hello, Alice. You are 30 years old.

File Handling:

• Read and write files: Learn how to open files with the open() function and how to read and write data with .read(), .readline(), .write(), and .writelines().

```
# Reading from a file
with open('example.txt', 'r') as file:
    content = file.read()
    print(content)
# Writing to a file
with open('output.txt', 'w') as file:
    file.write("Hello, file!")
```

• Handling File Contexts: Using the with statement to manage our file contexts makes sure that each file is closed when we've read or written its contents and doesn't linger around until the end of the program.

```
with open('log.txt', 'a') as file:
    file.write("Logging new entry\n")
```

4.2 Collections: Lists, Tuples, Dictionaries, and Sets

Each collection type serves unique purposes and has different properties regarding mutability and order.

• Dynamic arrays: Lists that can be reordered; with this type of collection, you can insert or remove items and change the elements. Useful for creating collections of things that change.

```
items = [1, 2, 3]
items.append(4)
print(items) # [1, 2, 3, 4]
```

• Tuples: Immutable, usually to return fixed sequences of data, faster than lists, data integrity is protected.

```
dimensions = (800, 600)
```

• Dictionaries: Mappings that expose two operations, an efficient lookup (in O(1) time) and insertion or removal. The value side can be mutable, as our needs don't require a sorted version. They are the most powerful way to construct a list that allows fast lookups.

```
phone_numbers = {'Alice': '555-1234', 'Bob': '555-5678'}
print(phone_numbers['Alice']) # 555-1234
```

• Sets: Unordered lists of unique elements – great for checking for membership, eliminating duplicates and mathematical operations such as unions and intersections.

```
colors = {"red", "blue", "green", "red"}
print(colors) # {'red', 'green', 'blue'}
```

4.3 List Comprehensions and Generator Expressions

One key to writing code that is so brief but so readable is that Python provides short syntax for defining both lists and generators.

• List Comprehensions: They provide a compact way of writing lists that result from an existing list. Each list comprehension consists of an expression followed by a for statement inside square brackets.

• Generator Expressions: These are like list comprehensions, but return generators instead of lists. Generators are lazy iterators: their elements are generated one by one and not stored in memory, so they are more memory-efficient than lists, especially for large datasets.

Chapter 5: Object-Oriented Programming

Firstly, it describes an object-oriented programming paradigm that centres around the idea of 'objects', which can encapsulate data, in the form of fields (often called attributes or properties), and behaviour, in the form of procedures (often called methods). In Python, OOP involves classes and objects that model things in the real world. This chapter covers the basics of OOP in Python, such as class definitions, inheritance and special methods and encapsulation.

5.1 Classes and Objects

Understanding classes and objects is crucial for applying OOP principles in Python.

Defining Classes and Objects:

• Syntax: Use the class keyword to declare a class by naming it and defining its body. Instantiate classes to create objects.

```
class Dog:
    def __init__(self, name, age):
        self.name = name
        self.age = age
    def bark(self):
        return "Woof!"
my_dog = Dog("Rover", 2)
print(my_dog.bark())  # Outputs: Woof!
```

• Attributes and Methods: Attributes are variables associated with an object, while methods are functions that define behaviours of an object.

5.2 Inheritance and Polymorphism

Code-reuse is made possible by inheritance, since new objects inherit properties of old objects. This means that it's easier to build an application, while maintaining it becomes simpler as well.

Inheritance:

• Base and Derived Classes An object of a derived class inherits attributes and methods from an object of a base class.

```
class Animal:
    def __init__(self, name):
        self.name = name
```

```
    def speak(self):
        return "Some sound"
class Dog(Animal):
    def speak(self):
        return "Woof!"
fido = Dog("Fido")
print(fido.speak())  # Outputs: Woof!
```

5.3 Special Methods and Encapsulation

We can also provide specialized ways of customising Python's default behaviour, and we can provide ways of hiding the internal representation, or state, of an object from the outside world.

Special Methods:

• Dunder Methods: __init__, __str__, __repr__, and others that allow emulation of built-in types or overriding operator behaviour.

```
class Book:
    def __init__(self, title, author):
        self.title = title
        self.author = author
    def __str__(self):
        return f"{self.title} by {self.author}"
my_book = Book("1984", "George Orwell")
print(my_book)  # Outputs: 1984 by George Orwell
```

Encapsulation:

• Private Members: Use an underscore (single or double) prefix (eg: _variable or __variable) to flag private attributes or methods as a means of indicating they shouldn't be accessed directly.

```
class Account:
    def __init__(self, owner, balance):
        self.owner = owner
        self.__balance = balance  # Private attribute
    def deposit(self, amount):
        if amount > 0:
            self.__balance += amount
            print("Deposit successful")
acc = Account("John", 100)
acc.deposit(50)  # Adjusts balance internally
```

Chapter 6: Error Handling and Exceptions

Any code has to handle errors, which is a fancy way of describing things that go wrong, where flow of a program. This ends up being an interesting part of any programming language – error handling – which Python uses exceptions for, and a few other forms of handling exceptional events. How to handle these properly is a crucial part of programming robust applications.

6.1 Understanding Exceptions

Unlike exceptions, however, they are something that a program can turn into a control flow – they can change the flow of control, with the help of Python. Exception handling is another story: exceptions are events that can deviate from the control flow of a program to handle an error or some other 'unusual' event.

Types of Exceptions:

- Python also contains some built-in exceptions – IOError, ValueError, ZeroDivisionError, etc – which are triggered automatically when something goes wrong.

```
try:
    f = open('file.txt')
    s = f.readline()
    i = int(s.strip())
except FileNotFoundError:
    print("File not found.")
except ValueError:
    print("Could not convert data to an integer.")
```

6.2 Handling Exceptions

You work with exceptions in Python with an exception-handling construct composed of blocks of try, except, else and finally. Your program will catch the error, do something with it, carry on or shut down orderly, depending on what you put in.

Exception Handling Mechanism:

• Try-except block: This is the basic building block of exception handling. You put the code that might raise an exception in the try block, and the code to execute if an exception is raised in the except block.

```
try:
    result = x / y
except ZeroDivisionError:
    print("Division by zero!")
else:
    print("Result is", result)
finally:
    print("Executing finally clause.")
```

6.3 Creating Custom Exceptions

Besides built-in exceptions, you can also define your own exceptions by writing a new exception class. For example, if you want to throw an exception for your business logic.

Defining Custom Exceptions:

• Custom exceptions are usually derived from one of the many built-in classes (such as Exception) or subclasses.

```
class MyError(Exception):
    def __init__(self, value):
        self.value = value
    def __str__(self):
        return repr(self.value)
try:
    raise MyError(2*2)
except MyError as e:
    print('My exception occurred, value:', e.value)
```

Thanks to what you've learned in this chapter, up to here, you now know how to handle errors and their exceptions in Phyton, and now you can code more solid and user-friendly Python applications.

Chapter 7: Interaction with the Operating System

Python comes bundled with many modules that let you interact directly with the operating system. This chapter will concentrate on using those modules to run system commands, work with the files and directories, and interact with running processes.

7.1 Shell Scripts and Automation

Python scripts can be used to automate the execution of various system administration tasks, for example, file backups, user management, system updates, etc.

Using the os and subprocess Modules:

• builtin os Module: A facility for operating system dependent functionality, for example reading or writing to a file system, managing paths, and executing shell commands.

```python
import os
# Get the current working directory
cwd = os.getcwd()
print("Current working directory:", cwd)
# Change the current working directory
os.chdir('/path/to/new/directory')
print("New working directory:", os.getcwd())
# Execute a shell command
os.system('mkdir new_directory')
```

• subprocess Module: Spawns a new process, connects to its input/output/error pipes, and returns its exit code. This is more powerful than os.system().

```python
import subprocess
# Run external command and get its output
completed = subprocess.run(['ls', '-l'], capture_output=True, text=True)
print('Return code:', completed.returncode)
print('Have {} bytes in stdout:\n{}'.format(len(completed.stdout), completed.stdout))
```

7.2 Accessing Files and Directories

Python's in-built libraries make it easy to work with files and folders; for example, creating, deleting, editing and navigating through folders.

File and Directory Management:

• Reading and Writing Files: use the open() function to open files and read or write data.

• Managing Directories: Use functions from the os module to create, list, or delete directories. As the example:

```python
# List all files and directories in the current directory
entries = os.listdir('.')
for entry in entries:
    print(entry)
```

7.3 Working with Processes and Threads

Python can also manage operating system processes and use threading for concurrency.

Process Management:

• Use the subprocess module for launching, controlling, and managing processes.

• Example of starting a process and reading its output:

```
process = subprocess.Popen(['ping', '-c 4', 'example.com'], stdout=subprocess.PIPE)
output, error = process.communicate()
print(output.decode())
```

Thread Management:

• Threading Module: Use Python's threading module to run multiple operations concurrently.

```
import threading
def print_cube(num):
    """function to print cube of given num"""
    print("Cube: {}".format(num * num * num))
def print_square(num):
    """function to print square of given num"""
    print("Square: {}".format(num * num))
t1 = threading.Thread(target=print_square, args=(10,))
t2 = threading.Thread(target=print_cube, args=(10,))
t1.start()
```

t2.start()
t1.join()
t2.join()

From the rest, this chapter retains the key skills necessary to interface with the operating system and control it using Python, which would prevent one from using the computer for the same purpose. In sum, Python is nothing more than a less time-efficient, more error-prone way of interacting with your existing system while at the same time providing too few additional instructions that are not achievable through other means.

Chapter 8: Web Development with Python

Python is a versatile programming language used for web development, from simple websites to web applications. This chapter will cover how to employ Python for web development, from the use of frameworks to web development with MVC architecture and creating APIs.

8.1 Web Frameworks: Flask and Django

Flask and Django are perhaps the two most popular web development frameworks in the Python ecosystem, and fulfil different needs, and scale from small to large applications.

Flask:

• Flask is a lightweight, flexible micro-framework that provides tools to build a web application but doesn't dictate how to architect it.

```
from flask import Flask, jsonify
app = Flask(__name__)
@app.route('/')
def hello_world():
    return 'Hello, World!'
if __name__ == '__main__':
    app.run(debug=True)
```

Django:

• Django: a high-level framework with an ORM, a routing system and a templating engine that fits best for complex, data-driven websites.

```
from django.http import HttpResponse
def home(request):
```

```
    return HttpResponse("Hello, Django!")
# In Django, the routing is handled through a URLconf, which is set up
in the project's settings.
```

The MVC pattern in web development divides the logic of the different parts of an application so as to ease management and scaling.

Implementing MVC in Python:

• Model: Specifies data structures and manages the database. In Django, models are defined as Python classes.

• View: Handles the presentation of data. Flask and Django use templates to render views.

• Controller: Mediates interactions between the model and view, routing the flow of data and responding to user input. In Flask and Django, this is the view function.

8.3 APIs and Web Services

That's the challenge of writing APIs, a standard situation in modern web development, where applications talk business to each other via HTTP requests.

Building APIs:

- Flask or Django can be used with extensions like Flask-RESTful or Django REST framework to create RESTful APIs.

```
from flask_restful import Resource, Api
app = Flask(__name__)
api = Api(app)
class HelloWorld(Resource):
    def get(self):
        return {'hello': 'world'}
api.add_resource(HelloWorld, '/')
if __name__ == '__main__':
    app.run(debug=True)
```

Such a setup is great both for microservices and for applications that interface with other services over the web.

Chapter 9: Data Science and Machine Learning

Because of the extensive number of libraries and frameworks available, Python is increasingly the language of choice for data science and machine learning. All of the most common libraries and frameworks will be covered in this chapter. If you are doing any sort of data science viz, it's likely that you'll need to use the NumPy, pandas and scikit-learn libraries. There are also some great visualisation tools available in Matplotlib and Seaborn.

9.1 Data Science Libraries: NumPy and pandas

NumPy:

• Overview: NumPy is the fundamental package needed for scientific computing in Python, providing a fast multi dimensional array object and tools to work with these arrays.

```python
import numpy as np
# Creating a NumPy array
array = np.array([1, 2, 3, 4, 5])
print("Array:", array)
# Performing operations
print("Mean of the array:", np.mean(array))
```

pandas:

• Overview: pandas provides high-rank data structures and facilities for working with numerical tables and time series, built on NumPy. It helps in data manipulation and analysis with more expressiveness.

```python
import pandas as pd
# Creating a DataFrame
```

```
data = {'Name': ['John', 'Anna', 'James'], 'Age': [28, 24,
35]}
df = pd.DataFrame(data)
print("DataFrame:\n", df)
# Accessing data
print("Ages:\n", df['Age'])
```

9.2 Introduction to Machine Learning with scikit-learn

scikit-learn:

• Overview: scikit-learn is a simple and efficient tool for data mining and data analysis, built on NumPy, SciPy, and matplotlib, and offers a wide variety of supervised and unsupervised learning algorithms via an easy-to-use interface.

```
from sklearn.ensemble import RandomForestClassifier
from sklearn.datasets import make_classification
# Generating a dataset
X, y = make_classification(n_samples=100, n_features=4, random_state=42)
# Creating and training a model
clf = RandomForestClassifier()
clf.fit(X, y)
# Predicting
predictions = clf.predict(X)
print("Predictions:", predictions)
```

9.3 Data Visualization with Matplotlib and Seaborn

Matplotlib:

• Overview: Matplotlib is an extensive library for creating static, animated or interactive visualisation in Python.

```python
import matplotlib.pyplot as plt
# Simple plot
plt.plot([1, 2, 3, 4, 5], [1, 4, 9, 16, 25])
plt.ylabel('Squared Values')
plt.xlabel('Values')
plt.show()
```

Seaborn:

• Overview: Seaborn's plotting functions are built on top of Matplotlib, and integrate well with pandas data structures, providing a convenient, high-level interface for drawing attractive and informative statistical graphics.

```python
import seaborn as sns
sns.set_theme(style="darkgrid")
# Using the same DataFrame as above
sns.lineplot(data=df, x='Name', y='Age')
plt.show()
```

This chapter shows how Python can be used for real-world, powerful data science and machine learning applications, focusing on pivotal toolkits and libraries.

Chapter 10: Next Steps and Community Resources

Once you've wrapped your mind around the fundamentals and intermediate topics of the language, the path forward demands constant learning and keeping fresh on the technologies and tools that make up the Python ecosystem. This last chapter points out some of the best practices, offers pointers to the Python community, and provides resources for continued learning and professional development.

10.1 Best Practices and Coding Standards

Learning and applying best practices and coding standards helps you write clean, efficient and maintainable Python code.

• PEP 8: Read PEP 8, the official style guide for Python, and learn how to format your code according to how the Python community expects to see it. PEP 8 will ensure that your code is readable and consistent with other Python projects.

• Code Reviews: Regular code review is essential to ensure high quality code, catch bugs early, share knowledge and promote quality standards, team collaboration and continuous improvement.

10.2 Participating in the Python Community

Being involved in the Python community can be enriching, offering educational opportunities, chances for professional networking, and giving back to open-source projects.

• Conferences and Meetups: Attend Python conferences such as PyCon, meetups and workshops to meet other Python developers and enthusiasts.

• Contributing to open source. If you are trying to learn to write Python, consider contributing to open-source Python projects. By working on a real-world problem, contributing to open-source will help you develop your skills and get feedback from the community. We all use open-source software, so you will be contributing to the functionality of the software that millions of people use.

10.3 Resources for Continued and Advanced Learning

As your knowledge of Python grows, you will want to explore advanced learning resources and keep up with new tools and libraries.

• Advanced Books and Online Courses: If you are interested in more advanced topics, have a look at advanced Python books and take online courses covering specialised subjects such as machine learning, data science, web development and the like.

• Co-create: Visit online communities (eg, Stack Overflow, GitHub), and expert-maintained blogs to learn from these and observe community discussions, projects, and articles.

10.4 Engaging with New Technologies

Python, the Swiss army knife of the tech world, is being applied in fields such as artificial intelligence, the Internet of Things and more.

- IoT Projects: Python is a good choice of language for IoT projects (Internet of Things), because it's readily readable, and has many rich libraries to collect and process data.

- AI and Machine Learning: Python has the most extensive machine learning libraries, such as TensorFlow and PyTorch, which power the recent boom in AI research and development. Becoming involved with these technologies can open up many career opportunities.

This final chapter concludes the book, but it doesn't mark the end of your journey with Python. There are plenty of ways to continue learning or taking your Python expertise to the next level, whether that's through taking courses, working within the Python community or applying for new jobs.

www.ingramcontent.com/pod-product-compliance
Lightning Source LLC
Chambersburg PA
CBHW050244230526
45470CB00005B/2101